Unlocking th

Five Keys for
Biblical Interpretation

Jeremy Corley

LITURGICAL PRESS
Collegeville, Minnesota

www.litpress.org

Cover design by David Manahan, O.S.B.

1   2   3   4   5   6   7   8

Library of Congress Cataloging-in-Publication Data

Corley, Jeremy.
    Unlocking the Gospels : five keys for biblical interpretation /
Jeremy Corley.
        p.   cm.
    ISBN 0-8146-2897-4 (alk. paper)
    1. Bible—Hermeneutics.   I. Title.

BX476.C63   2004
220.6'01—dc22

                                                    2003021133

Introduction

In 1993 the Pontifical Biblical Commission published a document entitled *The Interpretation of the Bible in the Church* (henceforth *IBC*). A British scholar named Leslie Houlden hailed this work as "perhaps the most remarkable and encouraging document to come from authorities within the Roman Catholic Church since the Second Vatican Council" (Houlden 1995, vii). Significantly, the document consolidates the advances in Roman Catholic biblical scholarship, particularly since Pope Pius XII's 1943 letter *Divino Afflante Spiritu* and Vatican II's 1965 Decree on Sacred Scripture *Dei Verbum*. Indeed, it goes further than them in explicitly offering a generally positive evaluation of most of the modern methods of critical biblical study.

Yet since its publication, I fear it has not had a huge impact on Catholic biblical interpretation in English-speaking countries. Various reasons may be suggested. For many professional biblical scholars the document may appear too brief and simplistic. For many pastors the document may be too densely written, lacking specific examples, while for many lay people untrained in theology the vocabulary and presentation may be too complex.

Friends of mine have requested an explanatory text to make the document's insights clearer to readers of the Bible. When teaching Scripture to students, I have found Section I of the document, outlining various methods of biblical interpretation, particularly useful. Accordingly, this booklet seeks to make Section I accessible to the interested reader. The booklet is an update of an article I published previously in a British journal (Corley 2000), by kind permission of the journal's editor.

In order to assist those who use Scripture for teaching, preaching, or personal study and prayer, this booklet briefly outlines the various methods of biblical interpretation as presented in Section I of the document, adding illustrations from the New Testament (especially the widow's mites story). Apart from a brief discussion of the spiritual interpretation of Scripture, this booklet will not deal with the document's other three sections that concern hermeneutical questions, characteristics of Catholic interpretation, and the interpretation of the Bible in the life of the Church.

The biblical quotations in this booklet are from the New Revised Standard Version (NRSV). Short references to books and articles are given in parentheses (e.g., Corley 2000); full details appear in the *Suggestions for Further Reading* at the end of the booklet.

The Five Methods of Biblical Interpretation

Readers of the Gospels will find wonderful stories, such as Jesus' appearance to his disciples on the road to Emmaus. The Gospels also include many marvelous parables, such as the Prodigal Son or the Good Samaritan. Moreover, there is much inspiring ethical teaching, as in the Sermon on the Mount. And most significant for believers, there is the Good News of Jesus' death and resurrection.

Anyone exploring the Scriptures will see the importance of knowing the historical background, as well as appreciating the literary qualities present. Delving deeper, it can be interesting and instructive to see how others have interpreted the texts, while psychological insights are also valuable. Finally, it is clear that many readers see the relevance of the texts to problems in today's society. Thus, five major approaches to the Scriptures are available, and biblical scholars who have explored these approaches offer five keys for opening up the riches of the Scriptures. The first section of the *IBC* document, entitled "Methods and Approaches for Interpretation" (34–72), lists these five keys or methods for gaining a better understanding of the Scriptures:

A. The Historical-Critical Method (Text-Critical, Source-Critical, Form-Critical, Redaction-Critical).

B. New Methods of Literary Analysis (Rhetorical, Narrative, Semiotic).

C. Approaches Based on Tradition (Canonical Approach, Recourse to Jewish Traditions of Interpretation, History of the Influence of the Text).

D. Approaches that Use the Human Sciences (Sociological, Cultural-Anthropological, Psychological).

E. Contextual Approaches (Liberationist, Feminist).

At the risk of oversimplifying, we could say that these five approaches correspond to the kinds of questions offered by five different sorts of people: a historian, a storyteller, a theologian, a care worker, and a justice advocate. It will become evident that when properly used, these five methods do not contradict one another, but rather provide an enriched vision, just as the comments of several people on a book or movie add up to more than the reactions of just one person (however insightful).

The document also refers to another category, fundamentalist interpretation (69–72). In my booklet I will say only a little about the fundamentalist approach, which the document sees as "dangerous" because it ignores the historical character of biblical revelation (72). Instead, I will make some brief remarks about the spiritual interpretation of Scripture, based on what *IBC* says (121–22).

My intention is to use examples to see how these five methods operate, from historical-critical study to recent contextual approaches (compare Brown 1997, 20–29). Rather than study each method in isolation, I will present the different approaches as applied to selected passages from the Gospels, so as to highlight the distinctive contribution of each method. As a regular scriptural example I have chosen the story of the widow's mites (Mark 12:41-44 and Luke 21:1-4). I have selected it for three reasons: it is short; it appears with differences in two Synoptic Gospels (though it is absent from Matthew); and it lends itself to modern sociological and contextual (e.g., liberationist and feminist) analysis. For easy reference I present the text of the story from the New Revised Standard Version.

> He sat down opposite the treasury, and watched the crowd putting money into the treasury. Many rich people put in large sums. A poor widow came and put in two small copper coins, which are worth a penny. Then he called his disciples and said to them, "Truly I tell you, this poor widow has put in more than all those who are contributing to the treasury. For all of them have contributed out of their abundance; but she out of her

poverty has put in everything she had, all she had to live on" (Mark 12:41-44).

> He looked up and saw rich people putting their gifts into the treasury; he also saw a poor widow put in two small copper coins. He said, "Truly I tell you, this poor widow has put in more than all of them; for all of them have contributed out of their abundance, but she out of her poverty has put in all she had to live on" (Luke 21:1-4).

A. The Historical-Critical Method

IBC asserts that "the historical-critical method is the indispensable method for the scientific study of the meaning of ancient texts," and since Scripture is the "Word of God in human language," its proper understanding requires this method (34). The name "historical-critical" is an ugly but descriptive term, as the method involves "criticism" (or analysis) of a text's "history." In other words, the method involves looking at the text with a historical perspective and in terms of its historical context. Although the method of "historical criticism" has sometimes been practiced negatively, so as to deny any historicity in much of the biblical narrative, such negativity is not inherent to the method, which can better be understood as "historical analysis."

Historical criticism of a biblical text usually involves four stages known by the jargon terms of textual criticism, source criticism, form criticism, and redaction criticism. In the following paragraphs I will briefly explain these four stages.

Textual criticism is a rather technical enterprise that involves establishing the most original textual form of the passage, particularly by comparing the most ancient manuscripts where they have differences in wording. In the story of the widow's mites, for instance, the two earliest Greek manuscripts of Mark 12:41 (Sinaiticus and Vaticanus) use the Greek word *kathisas*, "having sat down" (hence the reading of the NRSV: "he sat down"), whereas the word *hestōs*, "standing," appears in another early text (the Washington manuscript). Or to take another example, most manuscripts of John 1:34 end the verse with the words: "This is the Son of God," whereas some early copies of the text read: "This is God's chosen one."

In other cases, some manuscripts may include material absent from different copies of the text; for example, Mark 11:26 is absent from the earliest manuscripts and probably entered the later manuscripts under the influence of Matthew 6:15. The general rule is to prefer the readings in the earliest available manuscripts, and usually the shorter readings (since scribes might have added supplementary material).

Now we will look at the approach of source criticism. This method attempts to trace the source or sources for biblical material, whether earlier written material or traditions passed down by word of mouth. *IBC* elucidates this method as applied to the Gospels (35):

> To explain both the agreements and disagreements between the three Synoptic Gospels, scholars had recourse to the "Two Source" Hypothesis. According to this, the Gospels of Matthew and Luke were composed out of two principal sources: on the one hand, the Gospel of Mark and, on the other, a collection of the sayings of Jesus (called "Q," from the German word *"Quelle,"* meaning "source").

Because both Matthew and Luke follow the basic outline of Mark's Gospel (but with some changes and many additions), Mark is usually seen as the primary source for Matthew and Luke. Mark is generally dated around 65–75 C.E., with Matthew and Luke following a decade or two later. However, in the material not derived from Mark, both Matthew and Luke have many sayings in common, as is apparent from a comparison of the Sermon on the Mount (Matthew 5–7) with the Sermon on the Plain (Luke 6:20-49). These sayings are usually believed to come from a collection of Jesus' teaching (known as Q), from which both Matthew and Luke drew much material.

If we look at the story of the widow's mites in its two forms, the general opinion is that (as elsewhere) Luke here derives the story from Mark. Apart from a few stylistic changes, the wording of the verdict of Jesus in both Gospels (Mark 12:43-44; Luke 21:3-4) is very close. The strong likelihood that Luke has used Mark can be seen in the similar material preceding and following the widow's mites episode. In both Mark 12:38-40 and Luke 20:46-47 Jesus rebukes the scribes for their ostentatious religious practice, while in both Mark 13:1-4 and Luke 21:5-7 Jesus predicts the downfall of the Temple.

After considering the probable source of the narrative, we now examine its literary form or genre. *IBC* states that "genre criticism seeks to identify literary genres" as well as "the social milieu that gave rise to them" (38). The New Testament includes many literary genres, including prayers, letters, narratives, parables, genealogies, hymns, creedal statements, and apocalyptic revelations. A proper interpretation of a passage will consider its literary form. For example, parables (such as the Good Samaritan or the Rich Man and Lazarus) are not the same as historical narratives, so it would be a mistake to look for the inn of the Good Samaritan (though such a place is pointed out to present-day Holy Land pilgrims on the road down from Jerusalem to Jericho!).

Many scholars have identified the widow's mites narrative as a "pronouncement story," in other words, a story remembered for its punch line saying. This saying was evidently significant for the early Church. For instance, Vincent Taylor asserts that this story was told about Jesus "because it expressed his mind on the subject of almsgiving" (Taylor 1933, 73).

Closely connected with the literary form is the setting or context of the story in the life of Jesus. The question is asked whether the Gospel context accurately reflects the actual historical setting of the episode. A classic debate centers on the story of Jesus' "cleansing of the Temple": did it happen at the end of his ministry shortly before his death (so Mark 11:15-18), or did it occur near the outset of his public ministry (so John 2:13-22)? Although scholars have generally followed Mark's chronology, some authors would argue that John's chronology is more accurate here (Robinson 1985, 127–31).

After analyzing the literary form of the story and its life-setting, we can consider it from the viewpoint of tradition criticism. *IBC* declares: "Tradition criticism situates texts in the stream of tradition and attempts to describe the development of this tradition over the course of time" (38). We may illustrate this from the Lord's Prayer, which occurs in a shorter form in Luke 11:2-4 and in a longer form in Matthew 6:9-13. This traditional prayer, usually derived from the sayings collection known as Q, probably originated as a short prayer similar to Luke's version, but may then have been adapted for a liturgical context by means of expansions. For instance, the simple opening address "Father" (Luke 11:2) probably reflects Jesus' use of Abba to address God (Mark 14:36), but this form of address has been amplified to give the more suitable liturgical formula: "Our Father in heaven" (Matt 6:9). Similarly, the original conclusion, "Do not bring us to the time of trial" (Luke 11:4; cf. Mark 14:38) might suggest that God is the bringer of hardships for believers, whereas perhaps these difficulties would be better attributed to the devil (Jas 1:13). Hence in a Church context a new ending may have been added for liturgical use: "But rescue us from the evil one" (Matt 6:13). The development of the tradition did not stop with Matthew's text, because church communities felt that the prayer should end with praise of God, rather than with mention of the devil. Hence a doxology, already found with variants in the early second-century Christian writing called the *Didache*, was added in many later manuscripts: "For the kingdom and the power and the glory are yours forever. Amen" (footnote to Matt 6:13 in the NRSV). From this example we can see how one simple tradition has been expanded and developed, so as to meet the theological and liturgical needs of the early Church.

Now we will consider the approach of redaction criticism, the study of how the biblical documents were edited for a particular purpose in their final form. *IBC* states that redaction criticism "analyzes this final stage, trying as far as possible to identify the tendencies particularly characteristic of this concluding process" (38). The text is studied "with an eye to its character as a message communicated by the author to his contemporaries" (ibid.). When studying the Gospels, redaction criticism considers how the passage fits in with the general message of the particular Gospel writer.

Although the story of the widow's mites may have circulated separately as an oral tradition in the early Church, Mark has set it in a specific context which points up its meaning (and Luke has copied Mark in his placement of the story). While in Mark 12:40 Jesus has condemned the hypocritical scribes who "devour widows' houses" (presumably by using their religious authority to extract offerings from widows), here in Mark 12:43-44 Jesus acknowledges the widow's generous contribution to the Temple treasury. Whereas in Mark 13:1-2 Jesus predicts the destruction of the wonderful Temple buildings (presumably maintained partly through the offerings of poor widows), in Mark 12:43-44 Jesus recognizes the widow's generosity toward the maintenance of the Temple. When viewed in its context in Mark's Gospel, "the poverty of the widow will naturally be taken as due to a scribal devouring of her estate (v. 40)" (Gundry 1993, 729). The corruptness of the Temple, already equated with a "den of robbers" (Mark 11:17), yet maintained by the contributions of widows who cannot even afford to feed themselves (Mark 12:41-44), is presumably one reason for the Temple's predicted downfall in Mark 13:1-2.

The story of the widow's mites also contributes indirectly to Mark's portrait of Jesus. The widow (like the woman who anoints Jesus in Mark 14:3-9) is someone who gives all in the service of God. Her self-giving makes her like Jesus, who came "to give his life" as a ransom for many (Mark 10:45) and whose blood was "poured out for many" (Mark 14:24).

A redaction critical approach to the Lukan version of the story would observe that the Third Gospel has a special emphasis on women and on the poor. Like the generous women in Luke 8:1-3, who supported Jesus out of their own means, the self-sacrificing widow in Luke 21:1-4 gives (in a literal translation) "all the living that she had" for the upkeep of the Temple. Moreover, just as in the parable of Luke 16:19-31 the pauper Lazarus is to be exalted but the rich man is to suffer, so here the poor widow is honored but the rich benefactors are dishonored. Not for nothing does Luke 6:20 say: "Blessed are you who are poor, for yours is the kingdom of God," while Luke 6:24 says: "Woe to you who are rich, for you have received your consolation." In fact, F. Scott Spencer points out that Luke's two-volume work (the Third Gospel and Acts) includes six significant mentions of widows: Anna, the widow at Nain, the persistent widow, the poor widow, the neglected Hellenist widows, and the supported widows of Joppa (Spencer 1994, 718). Whereas the parable in Luke 18:1-8 depicts a widow persistently seeking to gain justice (presumably financial support), Luke 21:1-4 depicts another widow showing financial generosity to the Temple. In Luke's context, Spencer regards Luke 21:3-4 "not as a commendation of sacrificial giving to the Temple fund, but as a criticism of the corrupt Temple system which had just swallowed this poor widow's last penny and offered nothing in return" (Spencer 1994, 727).

The redaction critic would also consider why Matthew omitted the story found in Mark 12:41-44. A literary reason may be that in place of Mark 12:38-40, Matthew has collected his woes against the scribes and Pharisees into a block of teaching (Matthew 23) that leads straight into his discourse on the fall of the Temple (Matthew 24). A theological reason may be Matthew's view that in the person of Jesus "something greater than the Temple is here" (Matt 12:6), and hence the evangelist does not wish to support a place of worship due for destruction (Matt 24:2).

B. New Methods of Literary Analysis

Having looked at various aspects of the historical-critical method, *IBC* moves to a discussion of more recent methods of literary study (whether rhetorical, narrative, or semiotic). The document asserts: "*Rhetoric* is the art of composing discourse aimed at persuasion. The fact that all biblical texts are in some measure persuasive in character means that some knowledge of rhetoric should be part of the normal scholarly equipment of all exegetes" (42).

Clear examples of rhetorical skill occur in Luke's account of the defense speeches of the apostle Paul before King Agrippa (Acts 26:2-29). Paul begins the speech seeking to win the king's favor: "I consider myself fortunate that it is before you, King Agrippa, I am to make my defense today against all the accusations of the Jews, because you are especially familiar with all the customs and controversies of the Jews" (Acts 26:2-3). Later, in Acts 26:28, Agrippa acknowledges Paul's attempt to persuade him to become a Christian. Recent scholarship has also recognized many instances of Paul's rhetorical strategy of persuasion in his letters.

Narrative criticism is another form of newer literary analysis. *IBC* (45) explains:

> Particularly attentive to elements in the text which have to do with plot, characterization, and the point of view taken by a narrator, narrative analysis studies how a text tells a story in such a way as to engage the reader in its "narrative world" and the system of values contained therein.

An article by Elizabeth Struthers Malbon on the widow's mites story in Mark discusses narrative features of the story, such as the use of irony and the portrayal of characters (Malbon 1991). Malbon observes that Mark has connected the story of the poor widow's gift of her last two coins and the account of the unnamed woman's anointing of Jesus (Mark 14:3-9), since these stories are placed before and after Jesus' prediction of the downfall of the Temple (Mark 13). Malbon comments saliently: "One woman gives what little she has, two copper coins; the other gives a great deal, ointment of pure nard worth 300 denarii; but each gift represents self-denial" (Malbon 1991, 599). She adds:

> It is, of course, ironic that the poor widow's gift occurs in the doomed Temple; and it is ironic that the anointing of Jesus Christ, Jesus Messiah, Jesus the anointed one, takes place not in the Temple but in a leper's house (14:3), and not at the hands of the high priest, but at the hands of an unnamed woman (ibid.).

The narrative skill of the Gospel writer becomes apparent through his use of contrast and ironic juxtaposition.

Semiotic analysis, which is closely connected with structuralism, looks at symbolic relationships and significant structures in the text. This is a complex approach, deeply influenced by twentieth-century French philosophy and literary theory. *IBC* says that the semiotic or structuralist analysis of the text consists in "establishing the network of relationships (of opposition, confirmation, etc.) between the various elements; out of this the meaning of the text is constructed" (48). Thus, a structuralist analysis of the story of the widow's mites would take note of a primary contrast ("opposition") between rich and poor. The rich benefactors, who are publicly esteemed, are disparaged by Jesus, whereas the poor widow, despised and oppressed in society, is the one praised by Jesus. Thus, a reversal of values has taken place through the story: the poor despised widow has been lifted high by Jesus, whereas the rich Temple benefactors have been brought low (just as the beautifully adorned Temple will be brought low by its impending destruction, according to Mark 13:2).

C. Approaches Based on Tradition

After this review of three newer methods of literary analysis, *IBC* then considers three approaches based on tradition, starting with the canonical approach. As the name suggests, the canonical approach is rooted in the existence of an approved list ("canon") of sacred books, regarded by believers as the Word of God. *IBC* explains this approach:

> It interprets each biblical text in the light of the Canon of Scriptures, that is to say, of the Bible as received as the norm of faith by a community of believers. It seeks to situate each text within the single plan of God, the goal being to arrive at a presentation of Scripture truly valid for our time (51).

In the case of Old Testament writings, the canonical approach examines what it means for such texts to be read as Christian Scripture. For example, various New Testament passages regard Isaiah 53 (the fourth Suffering Servant song) as reaching fulfillment in Jesus' death and resurrection (e.g., 1 Pet 2:21-25).

A canonical approach to the New Testament would note, for instance, that there are four Gospels (not just one), indicating the possibility of at least four different ways of viewing the person of Jesus. Similarly, such an approach to the Beatitudes would take seriously the fact that Matthew 5:3 speaks of the happiness of the spiritually poor, while Luke 6:20 speaks of the happiness of the materially impoverished. The canonical method would also acknowledge that the Gospels report a variety of resurrection appearances of Jesus, on different days and in different places. Moreover, the fact that Mark 16:9-20 is in the Roman Catholic Lectionary means that it is regarded as a scriptural text, even though it is missing from the earliest manuscripts and was not part of the original text of Mark's Gospel.

Another possible approach to the Bible based on tradition is to pay attention to the Jewish traditions of interpretation. *IBC* comments that "the more astute Christian exegetes, from Origen and Jerome onwards, have sought to draw profit from the Jewish biblical learning in order to acquire a better understanding of Scripture" (54). Jewish tradition is helpful not only for interpreting the Hebrew Bible (which we share with the people of Israel) but also for understanding the New Testament, which arose in a Jewish environment and is full of Jewish customs and patterns of thought. For instance, Paul's discussion about the Law of Moses is often illuminated by Jewish thought. When Paul says that the Law "was ordained through angels by a mediator" (Gal 3:19), he depends on a Jewish interpretation of texts such as Deuteronomy 33:2-4.

Another aspect of attending to Jewish traditions is to view Jesus within the context of ancient Judaism (cf. Vermes 1973; Charlesworth 1991). Although in the case of many rabbinic texts, it is hard to offer a precise dating, these writings still illuminate Jewish patterns of thought, even when they are not the direct source of traditions in the New Testament. One example would be a Jewish parallel to the widow's mites story. This parallel occurs in a commentary on Leviticus called Leviticus Rabbah (*Lev. Rab.* 3.5), dating from several centuries after Christ:

> Once a woman brought a handful of fine flour [to the Temple], and the priest despised her, saying: "See what she offers! What is there in this [for the priests] to eat? What is there in this to offer up?" It was shown to him in a dream: "Do not despise her! It is regarded as if she had sacrificed her own life" (Boring 1995, 178).

An awareness of such Jewish traditions can save us from caricaturing ancient Judaism as an arid, hypocritical, or ritualistic system (Pontifical Biblical Commission, 2002).

A further approach based on tradition is to consider the history of influence of the text, especially within Christianity. *IBC* explains that "such an inquiry seeks to assess the development of interpretation over the course of time under the influence of the concerns readers have brought to the text" (56). A classic example would be to examine how the Christmas stories in Luke 2 and Matthew 2 have been interpreted. These key texts have been expounded and interpreted in liturgy and preaching, art and poetry, and music. Whereas recent biblical scholarship has emphasized their divergences, Christian tradition has often harmonized the stories. For St. Francis of Assisi, the Christmas stories emphasized the humble coming of Jesus among us in human flesh. The mention of the manger in Luke 2:7 was combined with the reference to ox and ass in Isaiah 1:3, and the story was brought alive by constructing the first Christmas crib in the Italian village of Greccio in 1223.

In similar fashion, but less prominently, the story of the widow's mites has also been interpreted in sermons for Christian audiences. Often the story's interpretation has served as an encouragement to charitable giving. Thus, in two of his homilies (10.13 and 52.5) the fourth-century preacher St. John Chrysostom uses the widow's mites story to plead for generosity in almsgiving. Elsewhere, the same story has been interpreted in a wider sense, to encourage a Christian concern for one's neighbor. For instance, St. John Chrysostom uses this text to insist that all Christians have the duty to help their neighbors. In Homily 20.4 Chrysostom declares: "Nothing is more frigid than a Christian who does not care for the salvation of others. You cannot plead poverty here: for she that cast in her two mites will be your accuser (Luke 21.1). . . . Everyone can profit his neighbor, if he will fulfil his part" (Phan 1984, 149).

D. Approaches That Use the Human Sciences

The *IBC* document next considers methods that use the human sciences, particularly sociology, cultural anthropology, and psychology. *IBC* says:

> The scientific study of the Bible requires as exact a knowledge as is possible of the social conditions distinctive of the various milieus in which the traditions recorded in the Bible took shape. This kind of socio-historical information needs then to be completed by an accurate sociological explanation (57).

A sociological approach to the widow's mites story would look at the social condition of widows in first-century Palestine. In an ancient patriarchal society without retirement pensions or state welfare payments, the widow would be dependent on the support of her sons or other male relatives. The frequent Old Testament exhortations to care for widows (Deut 14:29; Sir 4:10) and practice legal justice for them (Exod 22:22; Deut 24:17; Isa 1:17) suggest that many widows lived in poverty. Likewise, the early Church provision for the care of widows (Acts 6:1; 1 Tim 5:9-16) also points to the needy condition of many first-century widows in Jerusalem and elsewhere. Sociological analysis of the status of widows in society during the biblical period (see Hiebert 1989) emphasizes the deprivation and dependency of the widow, and thereby enhances the poor widow's generosity in the Gospel story.

Closely connected with the sociological approach to the Bible is the approach based on insights from cultural anthropology. Whereas sociological study tends to focus on economic or institutional aspects, anthropological study considers the wider cultural system. *IBC* explains: "In general, cultural anthropology seeks to define the characteristics of different kinds of human beings in their social context" (whether urban or rural), with "attention paid to the values recognized by the society in question" (60).

In an analysis of the widow's mites story, cultural anthropology would emphasize the social position of honor enjoyed by the rich donors by contrast with the low status of the impoverished woman. Indeed, the poor widow would be doubly disadvantaged in terms of her social prestige: as a widow in a patriarchal society she would not have a husband to maintain her honor, while as someone destitute she would lack the wealth that could bring her some social recognition (Malina and Neyrey 1991, 63). However, Jesus' statement reverses the social values by upholding the widow's honor at the expense of the prestige of the rich donors.

Having reviewed the approach from cultural anthropology, we turn to the more controversial area of the psychological approach. *IBC* declares that "the modern extension of psychological research to the study of the dynamic structures of the subconscious has given rise to fresh attempts at interpreting ancient texts, including the Bible" (61). The document goes on to give examples of psychological research, such as "to ascertain the meaning of cultic ritual, of sacrifice, of bans," as well as "to explain the use of imagery in biblical language" (62). Much recent attention has focused on understanding the concept of sacrifice, especially in response to René Girard's theory of sacred violence (Girard 1972). A psychological approach might point out the cultural violence whereby the wealthy Temple system exploited the generosity of such poor widows to support itself.

E. Contextual Approaches

After considering approaches from the human sciences, the document moves to contextual approaches, particularly those of liberation theology and feminism. A liberationist reading of the Bible is concerned to let the Bible speak to the people of today, particularly victims of oppression. *IBC* explains: "If a people lives in circumstances of oppression, one must go to the Bible to find there nourishment capable of sustaining the people in its struggles and its hopes" (64). Crucial for liberation theology is the view of God as Liberator: "He is the God of the poor and cannot tolerate oppression or injustice" (65). Such a view has practical consequences for biblical interpretation: "It follows that exegesis cannot be neutral, but must, in imitation of God, take sides on behalf of the poor and be engaged in the struggle to liberate the oppressed" (ibid.).

Writing on the use of the Bible in liberation theology, Jorge Pixley and Clodovis Boff connect the biblical paupers with the poor in Latin America: "We know of the *anawin* [*sic*] of the Bible: really poor and at the same time full of the greatest piety and trust in God. . . . Are the poor of Latin America not also a poor and at the same time religious people in the same way?" (Pixley and Boff 1989, 143). Later, they comment:

> Those who are really poor tend to have poor, humble and open hearts, while on the other hand, those who are rich tend to be more subject to arrogance, self-centeredness and envy. . . . This is not to idealize the poor, but simply to show how the poor relate to the divinity in reality (Pixley and Boff 1989, 146).

Thus, according to an optimistic liberationist reading, the poor widow would stand for the millions of poor and oppressed people who are not overwhelmed by their plight, but who manage to remain open and generous because of their whole-hearted trust in God.

However, a less optimistic liberationist reading might see the poor widow as a victim of an oppressive political and religious system. Addison G. Wright offers an interpretation akin to a liberationist reading:

> The story does not provide a pious contrast to the conduct of the scribes in the preceding section (as is the customary view): rather it provides a further illustration of the ills of official devotion. Jesus' saying is not a penetrating insight on the measuring of gifts; it is a lament. . . . Jesus condemns the value system that motivates her action, and he condemns the people who conditioned her to do it. . . . There is no praise of the widow in the passage and no invitation to imitate her, precisely because she ought not to be imitated (Wright 1982, 262–63).

A second contextual approach, which has grown in importance in recent years, is the feminist interpretation of the Bible. *IBC* distinguishes three types of feminist approach. In the first place, "the *radical* form denies all authority to the Bible" (67), and instead regards the biblical text as a cover for centuries of male oppression of women. In the second place, "the *neo-orthodox* form accepts the Bible as prophetic and as potentially of service, at least to the extent that it takes sides on behalf of the oppressed and thus also of women" (ibid.). In the third place, "the *critical* form . . . seeks to rediscover the status and role of women disciples within the life of Jesus and in the Pauline churches. At this period, it maintains, a certain equality prevailed" (ibid.). Leaving aside the radical feminist critique of the Bible, which in its most extreme form seems to leave little room for traditional Christian faith, let us attend to the neo-orthodox and critical approaches within feminism. According to Elisabeth Schüssler Fiorenza, for instance, the early Christian Church was originally an egalitarian community (see Gal 3:28), though it was later spoiled by hierarchical practices (Schüssler Fiorenza 1983, 140).

A feminist reading of the story of the widow's mites would focus on the woman herself in her context. While feminists would recognize her situation of social deprivation, they might differ as to whether she is a heroic protagonist or a victim of the patriarchal system. Thus, Mary Ann Tolbert offers a positive evaluation of the widow's action:

> Jesus' saying . . . underlines the ultimate or total nature of the financial sacrifice made by the widow. For one whose only protection from complete destitution is the little money she possesses, to give *all* of it to the Temple is to consign herself to disaster; yet this she does without fanfare or desire for glory, but out of faith (Tolbert 1992, 270).

Similarly, Joanna Dewey asserts: "Mark presents the widow, triply oppressed—female, without legal protection of a male, and economically destitute—as a model for discipleship" (Dewey 1994, 499).

By way of contrast, other feminist authors would assert that the widow's self-sacrifice indicates that she is a victim of the corrupt system of patriarchal values. Feminist authors have observed that by encouraging female self-sacrifice, Christianity has tended to foster the exploitation of women, who can easily become victims of male power. Such a feminist approach may shock those familiar with the traditional Christian ideal of self-sacrifice, but it may warn us that biblical stories can be misused to perpetuate the subservience of women. Indeed, the story of the widow's mites could be misused by men to propose an impossible ideal of total self-sacrifice for women, in support of a male religious system (represented by the Temple). Even if one disagrees with this radical feminist response, it serves as a challenge to traditional biblical interpretations of the widow's mites story, which can easily run the risk of complacent moralizing.

Fundamentalist Interpretation

In stark contrast to the challenge of radical feminist interpretation comes the fundamentalist approach. *IBC* explains that "fundamentalist interpretation starts from the principle that the Bible, being the Word of God, inspired and free from error, should be read and interpreted literally in all its details" (69). Although many people who begin to read the Bible may unconsciously have a fundamentalist outlook, a broader knowledge of Scripture can lead to a more nuanced perspective. While many fundamentalists may deserve commendation for giving serious attention to God's Word, a literalist approach is not the only way to take the Bible seriously, nor is it the best. In fact, a fundamentalist reading of the text tends to be rather "flat," not recognizing the diversity of traditions within the scriptural text (see LaVerdiere 2000). The *IBC* document criticizes fundamentalism for rejecting the insights offered by the various methods of interpretation outlined above.

We may illustrate the diversity of biblical traditions by looking at a person's attitude to material possessions. The widow's mites story could be understood to advocate the complete surrender of one's material possessions for the sake of God (see Luke 14:33), and we may compare texts that speak of giving everything to the poor (Mark 10:21; Acts 4:34-35). Yet other New Testament passages suggest that Jesus' first followers did retain some possessions. For instance, John 13:29 implies that Jesus and his disciples had a "common purse," which was used not only to help the poor but also to buy food (cf. John 4:8). Acts 11:29 speaks of the Christians in Antioch sending relief to the famine-stricken Judean believers "according to their ability," while in his encouragement to the Corinthian Christians to contribute to the poor, St. Paul does not ask them to give everything, but rather whatever extra they can afford (1 Cor 16:2). This brief discussion shows that while principles of financial generosity and self-sacrifice run through the New Testament, no single fixed viewpoint applies to each context, and a more varied interpretation provides a better understanding of the scriptural writings.

Spiritual Reading of Scripture

The five methods for studying the Scriptures do not exhaust approaches to the sacred text. Another time-honored approach is to use the Bible for spiritual reading, often known by its Latin title *lectio divina* (divine reading). Indeed, Vatican II's 1965 text *Dei Verbum* (n. 25) asserts that personal Scripture reading is important for all the baptized. The *IBC* text explains: "*Lectio divina* is a reading, on an individual or communal level, of a more or less lengthy passage of Scripture, received as the Word of God and leading, at the prompting of the Spirit, to meditation, prayer and contemplation" (121).

A twelfth-century Carthusian monk named Guigo II wrote a work called *The Ladder of Monks*, in which he outlined four stages of *lectio divina* (Magrassi 1998, 103–19). The first stage is *lectio*, the reading of the chosen passage of Scripture. Then the second stage is *meditatio* or pondering on the message of the biblical passage. The third stage is *oratio* or prayer in response to what God has communicated through the scriptural text. The fourth stage is *contemplatio*, the contemplation of God under the influence of the Holy Spirit. Modern writers sometimes add a fifth stage of *actio* or action, to carry out God's will as revealed during the course of the *lectio divina*. These categories do not need to be applied rigidly in every case, but those who practice spiritual reading often find this pattern helpful.

Someone praying about the story of the widow's mites might see her gift of everything she had as a prefiguring of Jesus' sacrifice of his life for us on the cross. The person might recall the prayer of St. Ignatius of Loyola: "to give and not to count the cost." Or a person might be reminded of the witness of martyrs who gave their lives for Christ, or saintly figures like Mother Teresa of Calcutta whose life was dedicated to the service of the poor. Each person's spiritual reading of this passage might lead to his or her own insights.

Conclusion

This survey of methods of biblical interpretation, as outlined in the *IBC* document, is intended to show how these various approaches may be applied to the biblical text, using the example of the widow's mites story. It is clear that there are many possible approaches to biblical interpretation, and that if rightly used, each method can help to illuminate the biblical text. The document encourages students of the Bible to explore a diversity of possible approaches, so as to gain insights into the riches in the scriptural text. The final page of the document issues a reminder that none of the methods of interpretation is an end in itself, but rather that all the methods are intended to serve the principal aim, which is "the deepening of faith" (130). My hope is that this booklet may contribute to a deepening of faith in the God for whom the poor widow in the Gospel gave up everything.

Questions for Personal Reflection or Group Discussion

1. Which of the five methods of biblical interpretation interests you most, and why?

2. Pick a favorite Gospel story and apply these five methods for understanding it. What insights do you gain?

3. What is the value, and what are the drawbacks of a fundamentalist approach to the Scriptures?

4. How does spiritual reading differ from these five methods of biblical study? Which is more beneficial for you? Give your reasons.

5. Practically speaking, how can we grow in our understanding of the Gospels?

Suggestions for Further Reading

Boring, M. Eugene, and others. *Hellenistic Commentary to the New Testament*. Nashville, Tenn.: Abingdon, 1995.

Brown, Raymond E. *An Introduction to the New Testament*. New York: Doubleday, 1997.

Casey, Michael. *Sacred Reading*. Liguori: Triumph, 1995.

Charlesworth, James H. *Jesus' Jewishness*. New York: Crossroad, 1991.

Corley, Jeremy. "Methods of Biblical Interpretation: A Guide." *Scripture Bulletin* 30/2 (2000) 2–15.

Dewey, Joanna. "The Gospel of Mark." In *Searching the Scriptures: A Feminist Commentary*. Ed. Elisabeth Schüssler Fiorenza. 2 vols. Vol. 2, 470–509. New York: Crossroad, 1993–94.

Fitzmyer, Joseph A. *The Biblical Commission's Document "The Interpretation of the Bible in the Church."* Subsidia Biblica 18. Rome: Pontifical Biblical Institute, 1995.

Girard, René. *Violence and the Sacred.* Baltimore: Johns Hopkins, 1972.

Gundry, Robert H. *Mark.* Grand Rapids, Mich.: Eerdmans, 1993.

Hall, Thelma. *Too Deep for Words: Rediscovering Lectio Divina.* New York: Paulist, 1988.

Hiebert, Paula S. "'Whence Shall Help Come to Me?': The Biblical Widow." In *Gender and Difference in Ancient Israel.* Ed. Peggy L. Day, 125–41. Minneapolis: Fortress, 1989.

Holy Bible: New Revised Standard Version, Catholic Edition. Nashville, Tenn.: Catholic Bible Press/Thomas Nelson, 1993.

Houlden, J. Leslie, ed. *The Interpretation of the Bible in the Church.* London: SCM, 1995.

LaVerdiere, Eugene. *Fundamentalism: A Pastoral Concern.* Collegeville: The Liturgical Press, 2000.

Leclercq, Jean. "Lectio Divina." *Worship* 58 (1984) 239–48.

Magrassi, Mariano. *Praying the Bible.* Collegeville: The Liturgical Press, 1998.

Malbon, Elizabeth Struthers. "The Poor Widow in Mark and Her Poor Rich Readers." *Catholic Biblical Quarterly* 53 (1991) 589–604.

Malina, Bruce J., and Jerome H. Neyrey. "Honor and Shame in Luke-Acts." In *The Social World of Luke–Acts.* Ed. Jerome H. Neyrey, 25–65. Peabody, Mass.: Hendrickson, 1991.

Muto, Susan. *Practical Guide to Spiritual Reading.* Denville, N.J.: Dimension, 1976.

Panimolle, Salvatore, ed. *Like the Deer That Yearns: Listening to the Word and Prayer.* Slough, Berkshire: St. Paul, 1990.

Phan, Peter C. *Social Thought.* Message of the Fathers of the Church, vol. 20. Wilmington, Del.: Glazier, 1984.

Pilch, John J. *Choosing a Bible Translation.* Collegeville: The Liturgical Press, 2000.

Pixley, Jorge, and Clodovis Boff. *The Bible, the Church and the Poor.* Tunbridge Wells, Kent: Burns & Oates, 1989.

Pontifical Biblical Commission. *The Interpretation of the Bible in the Church.* Rome: Libreria Editrice Vaticana, 1993. Also Boston, Mass.: St. Paul's Books & Media, 1993; Sherbrooke, Quebec: Editions Paulines, 1994.

Pontifical Biblical Commission. *The Jewish People and Their Sacred Scriptures in the Christian Bible.* Rome: Libreria Editrice Vaticana, 2002.

Powell, Mark Allan. *Fortress Introduction to the Gospels*. Minneapolis: Fortress, 1998.

Robinson, Bernard P. "The Uses of Scripture in the Church." *The Month* 259 (December 1998) 486–94.

Robinson, John A. T. *The Priority of John*. London: SCM, 1985.

Schüssler Fiorenza, Elisabeth. *In Memory of Her*. New York: Crossroad, 1983.

Spencer, F. Scott. "Neglected Widows in Acts 6:1-7." *Catholic Biblical Quarterly* 56 (1994) 715–33.

Taylor, Vincent. *The Formation of the Gospel Tradition*. London: Macmillan, 1933.

Tolbert, Mary Ann, "Mark." *The Women's Bible Commentary*. Ed. Carol A. Newsom and Sharon H. Ringe, 263–74. Louisville, Ky.: Westminster/John Knox, 1992.

Vermes, Geza. *Jesus the Jew*. London: Collins, 1973.

Williamson, Peter S. *Catholic Principles for Interpreting Scripture: A Study of the Pontifical Biblical Commission's "The Interpretation of the Bible in the Church."* Subsidia Biblica 22. Rome: Pontifical Biblical Institute, 2001.

Wright, Addison G. "The Widow's Mites: Praise or Lament?—A Matter of Context." *Catholic Biblical Quarterly* 44 (1982) 256–65.

Useful Websites

www.vatican.va

The Vatican website provides many Catholic Church documents, including Vatican II's short Dogmatic Constitution on Divine Revelation entitled *Dei Verbum* (1965) and the Pontifical Biblical Commission's documents on *The Interpretation of the Bible in the Church* (1993) and *The Jewish People and Their Sacred Scriptures in the Christian Bible* (2002).

www.ntgateway.com

This website, run from Birmingham University in England, is an access point for many good websites on the Gospels and other New Testament materials.